POPPER THE POLTERGEIST

THE FIRST HAUNTING SHOWN ON TV

BY MEGAN ATWOOD

CAPSTONE PRESS
a capstone imprint

Snap Books are published by Capstone Press, an imprint of Capstone.
1710 Roe Crest Drive
North Mankato, Minnesota 56003
www.capstonepub.com

Library of Congress Cataloging-in-Publication Data is available on the
Library of Congress website.

ISBN: 978-1-5435-7342-8 (hardcover)
ISBN: 978-1-4966-6614-7 (paperback)
ISBN: 978-1-5435-7351-0 (eBook PDF)

Summary: In February 1958, the Herrmann family began to experience strange events at their
home in Seaford, New York. The first occurrences were harmless—just caps popping off bottles.
But soon things escalated. Dishes were smashed, bookshelves toppled over, and objects moved.
Could these unexplained events have been the work of a devious poltergeist named Popper?

Image Credits
Alamy: PictureLux/The Hollywood Archive, 28; Getty Images: Eric VANDEVILLE/Gamma-
Rapho, 11, Hulton Archive, 13, Jon Shireman, 15, Nina Leen/The LIFE Picture Collection, 9,
10, 12, 17, 20, 25, Paul Slade/Paris Match, 5, 7, 19; Mary Evans Picture Library: John Cutten,
23; Shutterstock: avtk, Design Element, Chantal de Bruijne, Design Element, Featureflash
Photo Agency, 27, Fer Gregory, Cover, Giraphics, Design Element, GoMixer, Design Element,
MagicDogWorkshop, Design Element, NikhomTreeVector, Design Element

Editorial Credits
Editor: Eliza Leahy; Designers: Lori Bye and Brann Garvey;
Media Researcher: Tracy Cummins; Production Specialist: Kathy McColley

Direct Quotations
page 9: https://www.huffpost.com/entry/poltergeist-amityville-horror-survivor-real-
fear_n_1335948

Printed and bound in the USA. PA99

TABLE OF CONTENTS

UNEXPLAINED EVENTS

Detective Joseph Tozzi took notes at the Herrmann family's kitchen table, hardly believing his ears. The Herrmanns told an incredible story. For about a month, strange things had been happening in their home. Bottles had been popping open, things were being thrown by unseen hands, and furniture was moving—seemingly on its own. It all sounded ridiculous. Detective Tozzi was a **skeptic**. He did not believe in the **paranormal**.

But soon Tozzi's beliefs were challenged. As he stood in the Herrmanns' house trying to make sense of the story, a globe whizzed down the hall, almost knocking him over. At the same time in a different part of the house, the Herrmanns' son, Jimmy, saw a record player fly across the room. And another thing happened right then: A bookcase in a different room fell down.

The Herrmann home was located in a suburb about 30 miles away from New York City.

Everyone in the house had either witnessed the events themselves or had been standing right by the detective. There was no one to blame.

What could be causing this? Detective Tozzi had no idea. But others were convinced that the Herrmann family was being haunted by a **poltergeist**.

CHAPTER ONE

THE HERRMANN FAMILY

James and Lucille Herrmann lived a pretty average life for many years. James worked for Air France in New York City, and Lucille was a nurse. They had two children. Lucy was thirteen years old, and Jimmy was twelve years old. They lived about thirty miles away from New York City in a 1950s ranch-style house in Seaford on Long Island.

But their peaceful existence came to an abrupt end on February 3, 1958. It was a normal Monday for the Herrmanns. As usual, Mrs. Herrmann was home to greet their kids after school. But soon after Lucy and Jimmy had settled in at home, all three of them claimed to hear loud popping noises coming from several different rooms at once.

The Herrmann family's experiences would eventually be covered in a March 1958 *Life* magazine article and on many other news outlets.

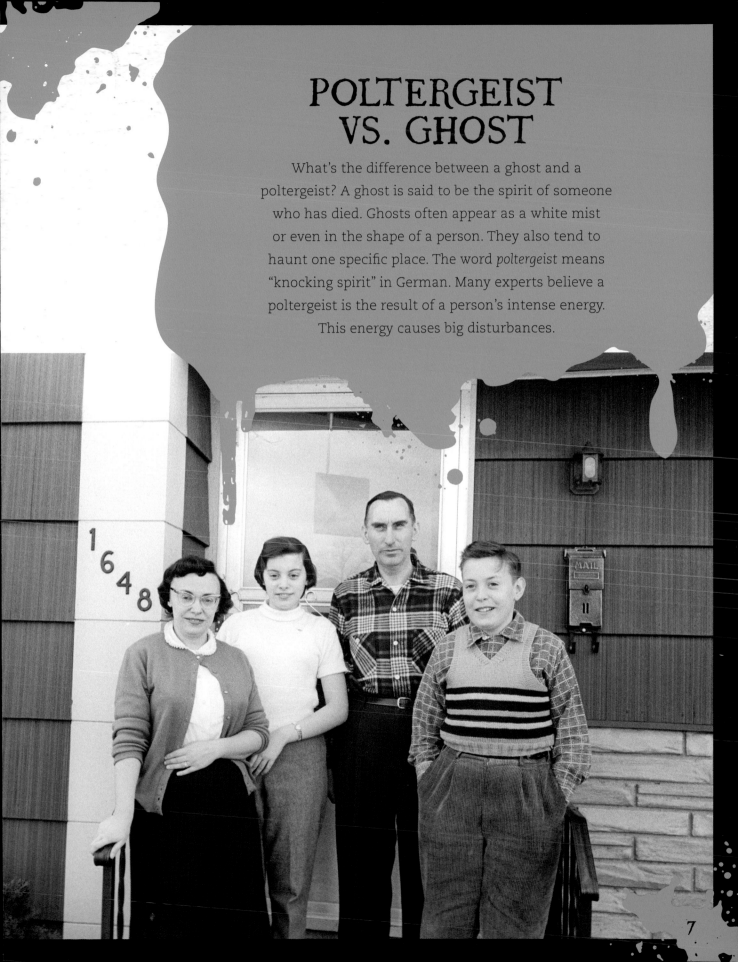

POLTERGEIST VS. GHOST

What's the difference between a ghost and a poltergeist? A ghost is said to be the spirit of someone who has died. Ghosts often appear as a white mist or even in the shape of a person. They also tend to haunt one specific place. The word *poltergeist* means "knocking spirit" in German. Many experts believe a poltergeist is the result of a person's intense energy. This energy causes big disturbances.

STRANGE THINGS

The sounds happened again: *POP POP POP POP*.

Bottles all through the house had popped their lids off. In the bathroom, a shampoo bottle popped its lid, as did a bottle of medicine. In the kitchen, the lid on a bottle of starch also popped off. A bottle of **holy water** in Mr. and Mrs. Herrmann's bedroom popped its lid as well. The bottle rolled around, spilling the liquid everywhere.

When the family went to investigate, they found that the spills from the bottles were fresh. But the strangest part of all—the lids were all screw-on. They would have to be turned several times to pop off.

At first, Mrs. Herrmann was more confused than frightened. She decided to call her husband to see if he knew what could have happened.

FACT

Holy water is water that has been blessed by a priest. It is largely used by people who are Catholic, like the Herrmanns. Holy water is especially used as protection from evil.

8

Lucy Herrmann said that her parents attempted to keep everything "as normal as possible when you have flying objects in your house."

SKEPTIC'S NOTE

It is possible to make a bottle cap pop off with only air pressure. However, the bottle would need to be empty. There is no record of whether there were any empty bottles in the Herrmann house that popped their lids.

CHAPTER TWO

THE POPPING DOESN'T STOP

Mr. Herrmann was at work when he received the strange call from his wife about bottles popping around their house. Mr. Herrmann was as confused as his wife. He asked if anyone had been hurt. Mrs. Herrmann said no, and Mr. Herrmann decided he would not leave work early. It was a weird occurrence, but nothing to worry about.

By the time Mr. Herrmann returned home that night, things had gone back to normal. In fact, things stayed normal for a few more days.

James Herrmann initially thought the popping could be a result of humidity.

But then on Thursday, February 6, the exact same thing happened at the exact same time. Mrs. Herrmann, Lucy, and Jimmy sat in the living room, and *POP POP POP* sounded through the house. The same thing happened again on Friday afternoon, February 7.

Mr. Herrmann still hadn't witnessed any of the bottles popping. But on Sunday, February 9, when Mr. Herrmann was home from work, the holy water in the bedroom **allegedly** popped open. The starch and turpentine in the basement also popped open. Now Mr. Herrmann understood what his family was talking about.

MORE MYSTERIOUS EVENTS

In 2004, the entire town of Canneto in Sicily, Italy, experienced fires in their homes that seemed to start out of nowhere. It happened again in 2014. A man was eventually arrested in connection with the 2014 fires, but many people still believe these were paranormal events.

The fires in 2004 started in January and took place over the course of five weeks, only to start up again in April.

A PERSON TO BLAME

Though the events seemed to be paranormal, Mr. Herrmann wasn't convinced. He suspected his son, Jimmy, who was interested in science, had somehow made the lids pop off. He decided to watch his son more closely.

For the next few days, Mr. Herrmann observed Jimmy as the strange popping kept happening. He looked for any pulley systems or clever tricks that could be causing the popping. But he found nothing. He finally decided he would ask Jimmy about it. He just knew that the popping was some sort of science experiment.

Jimmy's interest in science led his father to believe that he might've been pulling a prank with the popping bottles.

He confronted Jimmy in the bathroom. But as Mr. Herrmann looked on, a bottle of shampoo and a bottle of medicine moved on their own. When Mr. Herrmann investigated, he couldn't figure out any way Jimmy could have made that happen. Jimmy denied that he had anything to do with any of the strange events.

The Herrmanns believed their son. And they had had enough of these unexplained events. They called the police.

FACT

The Herrmann family lived only about five miles away from the house where another famous paranormal case took place. The Lutz family moved in to their house in Amityville in 1975, unaware that the previous owner had murdered his whole family. The paranormal events in the house included slime appearing on the walls and pigs with red eyes staring at the family from outside.

George and Kathy Lutz eventually told their story to author Jay Anson, who wrote the book *The Amityville Horror.*

Patrolman James Hughes came to the Herrmanns' home. He was very skeptical. Lids popping off? Things moving on their own? This sounded like a prank. But as he took down their story, Hughes saw and heard bottles popping open. He left thinking that something very strange was going on in the Herrmann household indeed.

After Hughes's report, Detective Tozzi was assigned to the case. The detective was certain this "haunting" could be explained away. He wondered if the whole family was simply imagining the events.

SEEING IS BELIEVING

On February 11, Detective Tozzi came to stay with the Herrmanns to witness the events himself. And right away, a perfume bottle spilled over. During the next few days, he witnessed several other events: objects falling over, lids popping off, and things moving on their own.

A lot of the activity seemed to center around the family's bottle of holy water. This lid popped off and spilled liquid out repeatedly. Strangest of all, the bottle felt warm to the touch whenever Detective Tozzi picked it up.

The detective was stumped. He had no idea what could be causing the strange events.

CHAPTER THREE

NO END IN SIGHT

The strange events in the Herrmann household seemed to be getting more violent.

On February 15, just four days after Detective Tozzi came to stay, the Herrmann kids watched TV with their cousin. As they sat there, a figurine on the end table suddenly rose up by itself and wiggled in the air. Then it allegedly shot across the room and crashed to the floor.

As usual, no one knew how this could have happened. So the Herrmanns turned to another **authority**: their priest.

Father McLeod of the Church of Saint William the Abbot came to the Herrmann house on February 17. He sprinkled holy water in every room and blessed the house. However, it seemed to do no good. Afterward, Detective Tozzi himself was almost hit by a globe. He also witnessed a record player fly across the room. The events were only getting worse.

By this time, all types of media outlets had picked up the story. News of the Herrmanns and their poltergeist was spreading quickly.

Reporters came from all over the world to witness the events that the Herrmann family was experiencing.

CELEBRITY STATUS

Television news stations began to report on the occurrences. A popular TV series called *Armstrong Circle Theater* brought cameras to the Herrmanns' house to tape the events. Nothing happened directly on camera. But the aftermath of the events was captured on film, such as interviews with witnesses and a dent in a wall caused by a thrown object. The film was considered to be the first televised haunting. The press gave their poltergeist a name: Popper.

The Herrmanns were bombarded with letters, calls, and visits. The phone rang all day and night. At one point, they received about seventy-five calls a day. Letters to the Herrmanns often suggested ideas about what was going on in their home. Some thought the events were caused by aliens. Others thought the Herrmanns had brought it on themselves somehow. Many people accused the Herrmanns of making everything up.

SKEPTIC'S NOTE

Many famous paranormal events turned out to be **hoaxes.** One example is a supposed fairy sighting in England, called the Cottingley Fairies. In 1917, cousins Frances Griffith and Elsie Wright claimed to have photographed fairies. It wasn't until 1983 that the photographs were finally **debunked.**

One man visited their house and prayed in the middle of the living room floor. Then he pronounced the house clean. Unfortunately, this was not the case. Detective Tozzi read the letters and answered the calls. He looked for anything that might help the investigation. He still believed there had to be some sort of **logical** explanation for what was happening to the Herrmanns.

Jimmy claimed he was sitting in the dining room doing homework when out of the corner of his eye he saw a record player fly across the living room.

MORE EXPERTS

As the calls and letters kept coming, Detective Tozzi considered several possibilities. He thought maybe the events could have been caused by **sonic booms** from airplanes overhead. But experts ruled out this possibility.

Tozzi also explored the idea that radio wave **frequencies** were causing the events. He thought perhaps the radio waves somehow moved the objects in the house. But a truck sent from the Radio Corporation of America didn't find anything unusual.

Robert Zider, a physicist, came to the house to see if he could find an explanation. Physicists are scientists who study the natural world to see how things work. Dr. Zider thought underground streams could have caused some strange magnetic occurrences in the house. He used a special tool to locate any streams and detect magnetic fields. But he found nothing out of the ordinary.

Detective Tozzi asked four different engineers to visit the house. All of them did, and none of them found anything unusual.

The reason for all the strange events, it seemed, would remain a mystery. Meanwhile, Popper continued to get worse.

Looking for answers, Detective Tozzi considered all possible explanations for the strange events.

CHAPTER FOUR

DIGGING DEEPER

By this time, the events happening in the Herrmann household had reached a peak. A sugar bowl rose and crashed on the floor. A bottle of ink smashed against a wall. Detective Tozzi was concerned about how violent the occurrences had become.

On February 24, a reporter named David Kahn from *Newsday* newspaper on Long Island stayed with the family. Another journalist, John Gold, from the *London Evening News*, watched as the **flashbulbs** for his camera lifted up and shattered. He also saw a centerpiece fly across the room into a cupboard.

Around that same time, news of Popper had attracted the attention of a famous **parapsychologist**, Dr. J. Gaither Pratt from Duke University. Parapsychologists are scientists who study paranormal events. Dr. Pratt and his colleague Dr. William Roll came to visit the Herrmanns on February 25.

POLTERGEISTS ABROAD

Popper isn't the only famous poltergeist. A case from England made headlines in the 1970s—the Thornton Heath poltergeist. In this case, a family was **terrorized** by a poltergeist for four full years. The family who lived in the house reported strange events. Music blared from radios. Objects were hurled across the room, often hitting people. Furniture crashed to the floor. Even after having the house blessed, the family found no relief. Finally, they moved out of the house. Those who lived in it after them reported no strange activity.

The scientists stayed in the house for the next three days. But Popper had decided to become quiet. The events stopped completely. The doctors left on February 28, never having experienced Popper's performance.

Dr. Pratt was a leader in the field of parapsychology. In 1960, he became president of the Parapsychological Association.

AN ANSWER?

Though Dr. Pratt and Dr. Roll had not seen any of the activity, many others had. The doctors believed the family and other witnesses. The doctors noticed, however, that Jimmy was always around when the events happened. They believed the young boy had accidentally caused the events.

In their work, the doctors had found rare cases where an **adolescent** had caused seemingly impossible things to happen with the strength of their feelings. They believed the **turmoil** that adolescents experience could turn into strange events, like the ones that were occurring at the Herrmanns' house.

SKEPTIC'S NOTE

Parapsychology is not a fully accepted field of study by all academic institutions or scientists. Many experts believe there is no scientific evidence of paranormal events.

Dr. Pratt observed Jimmy to determine whether he could be causing the events.

During their investigation into Popper, the doctors had found that Jimmy did have some anger with his parents. They believed him when he said he hadn't caused the disturbances on purpose. They also believed the eyewitnesses who said he physically couldn't have caused the events.

FACT

The ability to move things without touching them is called **psychokinesis.** Dr. Pratt and Dr. Roll believed this was how Jimmy had accidentally caused the events at the Herrmann house.

CHAPTER FIVE

THE LEGACY LIVES ON

After Dr. Pratt and Dr. Roll left the Herrmanns' home, Popper was quiet for two days. But then on March 2, the Herrmanns saw a dish crash to the floor. A night table in Jimmy's room fell over. And on March 4, a bookcase in the cellar tipped over, and a vase of flowers flew off the table and crashed on the floor.

Finally, on March 10, the family heard the now-familiar POP of a bottle. This time, it was the bleach in the laundry room. But that was it. The popping of the bleach would be the last time the Herrmanns received a visit from Popper.

Between February 3 and March 10, 1958, there were 67 documented instances of poltergeist activity in the Herrmanns' home. For more than a month, the Herrmanns had been terrorized by the strange events. But Popper the poltergeist had finally disappeared, and the Herrmann family was relieved.

HOLLYWOOD GETS INSPIRED

Popper was gone, but his **legacy** lived on. The strange events had captured the imaginations of the public. And then, they captured the imagination of a director and writer.

Steven Spielberg, a famous movie director and screenwriter, had read about the Herrmanns' experiences with Popper. From there, he got the idea for a 1982 movie named *Poltergeist*.

Steven Spielberg has won numerous awards for his work in film and directing.

The popular movie centers around an all-American family living peacefully in a suburb. Strange things begin to happen in the house. Chairs are moved, and furniture is knocked over. Objects smash against walls and the floors. This may sound familiar—these were things the Herrmanns had experienced.

To this day, no one knows for sure what caused the incidents in the Herrmann household. But the strange events they experienced lived on in the media. Popper, the first televised poltergeist in the United States, continues to thrill and intrigue audiences everywhere.

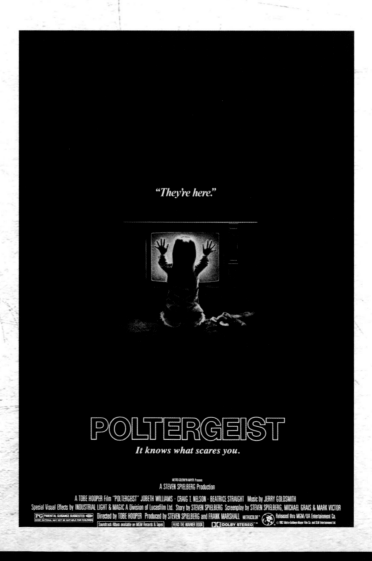

CURSE OR COINCIDENCE?

The movie *Poltergeist* had so much bad luck around the set that people started believing the movie was cursed. Dominique Dunne was the actress who played the oldest child in the movie, Dana Freeling. Dunne was murdered just a few months after the movie's release. Then the actress who played Carol Anne Freeling, Heather Michele O'Rourke, died at age twelve. The sequel, *Poltergeist II*, continued the bad luck. Two of the main actors died after the movie ended. Some people thought the curse came from one terrifying fact: In the first movie, the budget hadn't allowed them to make as many fake skeletons as they needed, so they used real ones instead.

FACT

Poltergeist was nominated for three Academy Awards. It is still a popular movie to this day.

GLOSSARY

adolescent (add-oh-LESS-ent)—a person between the ages of 10 and 19

allegedly (uh-LEDGE-ehd-lee)—said to be true or to have happened, but without proof

authority (uh-THOR-ah-tee)—a person who has some sort of power or command

debunk (dee-BUHNGK)—to expose as being false or exaggerated

flashbulb (FLASH-buhlb)—a light bulb that flashes while a picture is being taken, to give the picture good light

frequency (FREE-kwehn-see)—vibration that causes waves in the air

hoax (HOHKS)—a trick that makes people believe something that is not true

holy water (HOH-lee WAW-tur)—water that has been blessed by a priest

legacy (LEH-guh-see)—a thing or idea that lasts over time and is handed down to someone else

logical (LAW-jeh-kuhl)—reasoning that is clear and sound

paranormal (pair-uh-NORM-uhl)—something that cannot be explained by normal understandings of science

parapsychologist (pair-uh-sigh-KAH-luh-jist)—a scientist who studies paranormal events

poltergeist (POHL-ter-giest)—a supernatural force responsible for disturbances

psychokinesis (sike-oh-kin-EE-sis)—the ability to move things only with the mind

skeptic (SKEP-tihk)—someone who doubts or questions beliefs

sonic boom (SAH-nik BOOM)—a noise made by an airplane when it goes faster than the speed of sound

terrorize (TER-uh-rize)—to cause extreme fear

turmoil (TUR-moyl)—a feeling of confusion or agitation

READ MORE

Loh-Hagan, Virginia. *MacKenzie Poltergeist*. Ann Arbor, MI: Cherry Lake Publishing, 2018.

McCollum, Sean. *Handbook to Ghosts, Poltergeists, and Haunted Houses*. North Mankato, MN: Capstone Press, 2017.

Ramsey, Grace. *Haunted Objects*. Vero Beach, FL: Rourke Educational Media, 2016.

INTERNET SITES

All About Ghosts

https://www.cbc.ca/kidscbc2/the-feed/monsters-101-all-about-ghosts

Spooky Ghost Stories

https://people.howstuffworks.com/culture-traditions/holidays-halloween/ghost-stories.htm

Scary Podcasts for Kids

https://medium.com/kidslisten/spooky-for-kids-e1543b0eb82b

INDEX